THE
BRITISH
NATIONALITY
TEST

How British are you?

THE
BRITISH
NATIONALITY
TEST

2014/15

BRITAIN
AN EQUAL OPPORCHANCITY COUNTRY

First published 2014
by Black & White Publishing Ltd
29 Ocean Drive, Edinburgh EH6 6JL

1 3 5 7 9 10 8 6 4 2 14 15 16

ISBN: 978 1 84502 699 8

Illustrations by Oli Nightingale of Kartoon Factory

A CIP catalogue record for this book is available from the British Library.

Typeset by Creative Link, North Berwick
Printed and bound by Hussarbooks, Poland www.hussar.pl

CONTENTS

INTRODUCTION AND TEST GUIDELINES

APPENDICES

24 July 2014

Dear Candidate

A Message from the Examination Board

With the advent of global warming Britain is set to become a paradise with long, hot summers and short, warm winters. An Illustrated Guide to the New Britain follows this letter.

However, it is anticipated that this dramatic climate change will lead to an unsustainable influx of people into the country. To avoid this and the associated pressure on our land, resources and infrastructure, the authorities have agreed to introduce a formal immigration test for all aspiring British residents. Although the process may be daunting, it is believed that the British Nationality Test is the fairest way of managing a difficult situation.

It is anticipated that there will be places for a wide range of applicants, but priority will be given to those with the following skills:

Deficit reducers	Numerate bankers
Galacticos	Dieticians

This time round the following groups need not bother applying:

> Raindancers
> Dodgy DJs

Candidates should be assured that the decision to introduce the British Nationality Test is entirely driven by the climate-related issues facing the UK. In particular, this initiative is not a politically ingenious method of outmanoeuvring Britain's loons – swivel-eyed or otherwise – in the lead-up to the 2015 general election.

It is anticipated that competition will be fierce for a place in the New Britain and many will unfortunately be disappointed. And despite what the European Union's lawyers may say, the government regrets that we cannot accept more candidates. More specifically, and despite the forecast demise of Europe in the post-global-warming era, there will be a strict quota on candidates wishing to move to Britain from our immediate neighbours across the Channel.

We wish you well with the test and I hope that your many years of diligent study bear fruit.

Di Aspora

pp
Professor Rab Scallion
Chairman, Examination Board

POST GLOBAL WARMING: AN ILLUSTRATED GUIDE

With global warming almost upon us, the next few pages illustrate some of the more profound changes Britain can expect to see over the next few years. On the left-hand side of each page are photographs of the country as we know it now. And on the right-hand side are artists' impressions of the same scenes post global warming.

July in Skegness

Padstow Harbour

Outdoor Pursuits, West Country

Rochdale

Black Angus Cow, Devon

COMPLETING THE TEST

INSTRUCTIONS

- Candidates should at least attempt to read, if not understand, all the questions.
- Talking is encouraged, and please ensure that all mobile and digital devices are switched on.
- Candidates have two weeks to complete the test.
- To avoid burnout it is suggested that you only attempt one section at a time.
- Please only use invisible ink so that the test paper can be reused.
- Candidates may confer as they see fit, but this is unlikely to help.
- Marks may be dedacted for bad spelling.
- Due to ongoing austerity measures, candidates are responsible for marking their own paper.
- Candidates with any sympathy or connection to the EU should subtract ten marks for being ideologically suspect.
- Candidates with a weakness for cheese, wine, olive oil or garlic should subtract fifteen marks for having unsavoury culinary leanings.

BONUS OPPORCHANCITY

Candidates will also be asked to attempt a set of more advanced questions. These Bonus Opporchancities are clearly labelled throughout the paper. Subject to availability and the payment of a discretionary administration fee into our Turks and Caicos bank account (see our website for details), candidates answering one or more of these questions correctly will be granted some form of residency.

STREET TALK

In several sections candidates are asked to answer a set of Street Talk questions. These are designed to measure applicants' awareness and understanding of contemporary British life. To comply with the Data Protection Act, names of the actual commentators have been changed, for example:

'Immigrants have always brought something special to Britain.'
Nan Bread and Chris P. Duck

FREQUENTLY ASKED QUESTIONS

FAQs are listed in Appendix 2 and include guidance on several key aspects of the test and British warming, for example:

Q: Will the full English still be kosher?

A: Technically speaking, the full English has never been kosher. However, it is anticipated current culinary practices will continue but in London and the South-East French fries will be replaced by couscous.

ILLUSTRATIONS

For candidates whose first language is not English or who perhaps may even have some difficulty reading, the Examination Committee has added several illustrations to assist candidates in formulating their answers to the questions. For example:

Which British institution does the sketch below portray?

(a) House of Commons ☐   (c) UK Supreme Court ☐

(b) House of Lords*   ☐   (d) UKIP's AGM   ☐

*   as of October 2012

Seven Hundred & Sixty Shades of Grey
(& counting)

For your information the answer is (b), but it is understandable if you chose one of the other options.

THE GRADING SYSTEM

The pass mark is 50%. However, and irrespective of a candidate's scores in other sections, a candidate will also be expected to have scored over 80% in both Gender Studies and Modern Studies.

The higher a candidate's score, the more attractive the choice of location available to a prospective resident in New Britain. For example:

50%–60% Rhyl

61%–70% Macclesfield

71%–80% Liverpool

81%–100% Hackney

THE TEST PAPER

GENDER STUDIES

1.1 *Which of the following statements does not capture the attitude, behaviour and beliefs of the average British male?*

(a) To control the TV remote is to control the world. ☐

(b) Dirty dishes migrate automatically to the dishwasher. ☐

(c) Toilet rolls grow naturally on their holders. ☐

(d) An empty milk carton goes back into the fridge and not the bin. ☐

(2 marks)

1.2 *Judging by the text below, are you:*

(a) An old soldier ☐   (b) A lesbian ☐   (c) Both ☐

An old soldier, complete with a chestful of medals, sat down at Starbucks in Manchester, ordered a cup of coffee and started rereading his treasured copy of *The History of the Royal Fusiliers*. As he slowly sipped his coffee, a young woman sat down next to him.

She turned to the old soldier and asked, 'Were you a real soldier?'

He replied, 'Well, I spent my whole life in the Fusiliers fighting Germans, the Japanese and Communists, so yes, I am an old soldier. And you, what are you?'

She said, 'I'm a lesbian. I spend my whole day thinking about naked women. As soon as I get up in the morning, I think about naked women. When I shower, I think about naked women. When I watch TV, I think about naked women. It seems everything makes me think of naked women.'

The old soldier looked quizzically at the lady, nodded and then returned to his book.

A little while later, a young man sat down on the other side of the soldier, noticed that he was reading *The History of the Royal Fusiliers* and casually asked, 'Are you a soldier?'

He replied, 'I always thought I was, but I've just discovered that I'm a lesbian.'

(2 marks)

1.3 *From the passage below, was the wife of the Lake District man:*

(a) A rocket scientist ☐   (c) Flaxen-haired ☐

(b) A brain surgeon ☐

On a bitterly cold winter morning in Penrith, a couple were listening to the radio over their breakfast. It came as no surprise when the announcer said, 'The Lake District is expected to have eight to ten inches of snow today, so please park your car on the even-numbered side of the street to allow the council's snow plough to get through.' Immediately, the community-minded wife went out and moved her car.

Exactly a week later, the same radio announcer said, 'Cumbria is expecting eight to ten inches of snow today, so please park your car on the odd-numbered side of the street to allow the council's snow plough to get through.' The diligent wife went out and moved her car again.

The next week the couple were again having breakfast when the radio announcer said, 'We are expecting eight to ten inches of snow today, so—' Just then the electric power was cut. The wife was very upset and, with a worried look on her face, she said, 'Hugh, I don't know what to do. Which side of the street do I need to park on so the council's snow plough can get through?'

Then, with the love and understanding gleaned from twenty years or marriage, the husband gently replied: 'This time, love, why don't you just leave the car in the garage?'

(2 marks)

Bonus Opporchancity

1.4   *A recent Portavogie University survey on the attitudes of Belfast women towards their male companions provided many penetrating insights into the female mindset. Which of the following quotes are taken directly from this much acclaimed study?*

(a) 'The average Belfast male thinks he isn't.' ☐

(b) 'I asked my husband, "If you can't live without me, then why aren't you dead yet?"' ☐

(c) 'Belfast men do cry, but only when forced to do the ironing.' ☐

(d) 'For Belfast men, sex is the most beautiful thing that money can buy.' ☐

(2 marks)

1.5 *In the extract below, do you believe that Big Jack's concern is that 'hell hath no fury like a British woman scorned'?*

(a) Yes ☐   (b) No ☐

Rob was at work one day when he noticed that his mate Big Jack was wearing an earring. Rob knew Big Jack to be a conservative man and was curious about his sudden change in fashion sense, so Rob asked, 'What's with the bling? Surely you're a bit old for that?'

'It's no big deal, it's only an earring,' Big Jack replied sheepishly.

Rob let it lie there, but then his curiosity got the better of him and he asked, 'So, how long have you been wearing it?'

Reluctantly, Big Jack replied, 'Ever since the wife found it in the back seat of the car.'

(2 marks)

1.6 *Please study the illustration below and decide whether Relate is:*

(a) A distant relative ☐

(b) The new Farrow & Ball colour chart ☐

(2 marks)

1.7 *From the passage below, decide whether, when it comes to affairs of the heart, a Yorkshireman can be overly opportunistic:*

(a) Yes ☐   (b) No ☐

A notorious robber went into a bank in Leeds and demanded all its money. Once he was given the case, he turned to a customer and barked, 'Did you see my face?'

The man replied, 'Yes, sir, I'm afraid I did.'

Without hesitation, the robber pulled out a gun and shot the customer, killing him instantly.

He then turned to a couple standing next to him and asked the man the same question: 'Did you see my face?'

Instantly the man replied, 'No, sir, I didn't, but my wife did.'

(2 marks)

1.8 *Does the following statement accurately reflect the attitude, behaviour and beliefs of members of the men-only Pratt's Club in London and the men-only Muirfield Golf Club in Edinburgh?*

'God created women because sheep can't type.'

(a) Yes ☐   (b) No ☐

(2 marks)

1.9 *Saxon Singles is England's fastest growing online and newspaper dating service. From the following selection of recent 'male seeking female' adverts, candidates are asked to identify the ones that they believe capture the essence of the English male. A glossary of frequently used terms and acronyms is provided for candidates who may be unfamiliar with the language used by Saxon Singles participants:*

Saxon Singles: Some Frequently Used Terms

DDF Disease- and drug-free   FILP Fully index-linked pension

DG Damaged goods   MBA Married but available

DTM Desperate to meet

(a) DDF male, 45, Dudley area shelf stacker, seeks 20–25-year-old who puts out on the first date and is interested in fortified wine, Sky Sports, eating with her fingers and starting bare-knuckle fights in an empty room. ☐

(b) Bitter, disillusioned, flame-haired Dover-based bundle of mischief seeks wealthy lady for bail purposes. No retreads please. ☐

(c) Sub-prime MBA Sheffield man, 27, medium build, some brown hair, bloodshot eyes, seeks cast-iron alibi for the night of February 27 between 8 p.m. and 11.30 p.m. ☐

(d) Self-made man from Leicester with own caravan and FILP DTM equally sophisticated and solvent lady for long weekends in Great Yarmouth and to share the Calor Gas costs. ☐

(2 marks)

1.10 Is the average British male this quick-thinking?

(a) Yes ☐   (b) Even quicker ☐

Tucked away on Sir Philip William-Brown's country estate there was a small and secluded lake. Over the years, Sir Philip had lovingly stocked the lake with fish, sown acres of colourful wildflowers on the slopes overlooking the water and even planted an apple orchard on the lake's south-facing hillside.

One late summer evening, Sir Philip decided to go down to the lake to pick a few of his apples. On his way out of the house, he picked up a bucket to hold the fruit. As he neared the lake he was surprised but delighted to hear female laughter. When he walked closer he saw that a group of young female walkers had decided to go skinny-dipping.

Sir Philip coughed firmly but politely to make the women aware of his presence. Alas, when they saw a man the women screamed and swam to the far side of the lake. Then one of them shouted, 'We're not coming out until you leave.'

Sir Philip frowned and replied indignantly, 'I didn't come down just to watch you ladies swim or to see you naked.' Holding up his bucket, he continued, 'Actually this is my little lake and I'm here to feed the piranhas.'

(2 marks)

1.11 *After researching the TV series* **Top Gear,** *British scientists have discovered that the show's presenters all react unusually when they meet a woman wearing a leather dress. Their hearts beat faster, their throats dry up and they go weak at the knees. What do you think could be the reason for this unusual behaviour?*

(a) Leather naturally hugs the female form. ☐

(b) There is something intrinsically arousing about leather. ☐

(c) Women wearing leather always smell like a new car. ☐

(2 marks)

1.12 *Recent medical research suggests that the quickest way to an Englishman's heart is:*

(a) Through love and understanding ☐

(b) Through his stomach ☐

(c) Through his ribcage ☐

(2 marks)

TOTAL MARKS AVAILABLE FOR SECTION I: 24

THE CANDIDATE'S SCORE:

EUROPEAN RELATIONS

2.1 Does the following diplomatic incident illustrate that the European Union and the British will fight about anything and everything?

(a) Yes ☐   (b) No ☐

A pompous Brussels bureaucrat drove through a stop sign in London and got pulled over by a local policeman. The bureaucrat thought that he was much smarter than any local policeman and he decided to prove this to himself and have some fun at the Londoner's expense! The following exchange then unfolded:

London policeman	Licence and registration, please.
Brussels bureaucrat	Why?
London policeman	You didn't come to a complete stop at the stop sign.
Brussels bureaucrat	I slowed down and no one was coming.
London policeman	You still didn't come to a complete stop. Licence and registration, please.
Brussels bureaucrat	What's the difference?
London policeman	The difference is you have to come to a complete stop: that's the law in Britain. Licence and registration, please!
Brussels bureaucrat	If you can show me the difference between slow down and stop, then I'll gladly give you my licence and registration and you can issue your ticket. If not, you don't give me the ticket and let me go about my business.
London policeman	Sounds fair. Could you please exit your vehicle, sir.

Despite the inconvenience, the Brussels bureaucrat got out of his car and the policeman took out his baton and started vigorously hitting the man.

London policeman   Now, do you want me to stop or just to slow down?

(2 marks)

2.2 Does the incident reported below further weaken the already fragile diplomatic relations between Britain and France?

(a) Yes ☐   (b) No ☐

A Frenchman and a Brit were sitting around talking one afternoon over a beer. After a while, the Frenchman said, 'If I were to sneak over to your house and sleep with your wife while you were off golfing and she fell pregnant and had a baby, would that make us related?'

The Brit cocked his head sideways, squinted his eyes and, obviously thinking hard about the question, finally said, 'Well, I don't know about being related, but it would make us even.'

(2 marks)

2.3 What does the incident reported below tell you about how easily Britain's 'red top' press could further sour the already frayed diplomatic relations between Britain and France?

(a) Nothing changes ☐   (b) *Plus ça change* ☐

It was the England v. France International weekend in London and the crowd was making its way towards Twickenham when a Rottweiler suddenly lunged towards an eight-year-old English girl with long blonde hair and beautiful blue eyes. As the dog bared its teeth and attacked, most of the match-goers recoiled in horror, except for one brave man who jumped out of the crowd, grabbed the dog by the throat and throttled it.

As the match-goers cheered in admiration, a passing journalist who had witnessed the selfless act shouted to the hero, 'That was truly remarkable, I can see the headline now.'

English Rugby Fan Saves Young Girl from Jaws of Rabid Rottweiler.

But the hero's friend interjected. 'No, you've got it all wrong. He's not here for the rugby.'

'Don't worry,' replied the journalist, 'I can see the headline now.'

English Hero Saves Girl from Jaws of Rottweiler.

Finally able to get a word in edgeways, the reluctant hero replied, 'Sorry, but you're wrong again. I am not English, I am from Paris!'

'Don't worry,' said the journalist, 'I can see the headline now.'

French Bastard Strangles Much-Loved Family Puppy.

(2 marks)

2.4 *Please read the short passage below and decide what is the moral of the story:*

(a) Beware the ever-predatory French male ☐

(b) One good turn deserves another ☐

(c) Look before you leap ☐

A naive English girl was down on her luck and stranded in France and she finally decided to end it all by throwing herself into the cold, dark waters of Calais harbour. As she stood on the edge feeling sorry for herself, a young French sailor noticed her as he strolled by. 'I hope that you're not thinking of jumping, are you?' he asked.

'Yes, I am,' replied the sobbing girl.

Putting his arm around her, the sailor coaxed her back from the edge of the dock. He said, 'Look, nothing's that bad. Tell you what, we're sailing for America tomorrow. Why don't I help you stow away on my ship and then you can start a new life over there? I'll set you up in one of the lifeboats and bring you food and water every night. And I'll look after you if you look after me, if you know what I mean. You just have to keep very quiet so that you're not discovered.'

The girl, having no other option, agreed and let the sailor sneak her on board the ship that very night. For the next two weeks the sailor came to the lifeboat every night, bringing her food and water and making love to her. Unfortunately, during the third week the captain ordered a surprise lifeboat inspection. He peeled back the cover on the first boat, discovered the English girl and demanded an explanation. The girl immediately admitted the whole story. 'I've stowed away to begin a new life in America and one of your kind sailors is helping me out. He smuggled me on board, he brings me food and water every night and, as we say in English, he's screwing me.'

The captain listened in disbelief before replying, 'He certainly is, sweetheart. This is a Channel ferry.'

(2 marks)

2.5 ***Does the story below explain why the Empire was British and not French or, indeed, German?***

(a) Possibly ☐   (b) What a great idea ☐

An Englishman, a Frenchman and the German supermodel Claudia Schiffer were sitting together on a train. Suddenly the train went through a tunnel and the carriage was plunged into darkness (it was a British train). Then there was a kissing noise and the sound of a really painful slap.

When the train came out of the tunnel, Claudia Schiffer and the Englishman were sitting as if nothing had happened and the Frenchman was holding his hand against his face as if he had been slapped.

The Frenchman was thinking, 'The English guy must have kissed Claudia Schiffer; she thought it was me and hit me.'

At the same time, Claudia Schiffer was thinking, 'That French guy must have tried to kiss me but actually kissed the Englishman and got slapped for it.'

Meanwhile, the Englishman was thinking, 'Great, the next time the train goes through a tunnel I'll make more kissing noises and slap that Frenchman even harder.'

(4 marks)

2.6 Where do Germans tend to shoot themselves?

(a) In the foot ☐

(b) Between their eyes and right in their superiority complex ☐

(2 marks)

2.7 Is the difference between Frenchmen and toast the fact that you can make soldiers out of toast?

(a) *Oui* ☐   (b) *Non* ☐

(c) *Peut-être* ☐   (d) *Merde* ☐

(2 marks)

2.8 Candidates are asked to match the following three words to the three definitions presented below: trilingual, bilingual, British

(a) Someone who speaks three languages _____

(b) Someone who speaks two languages   _____

(c) Someone who speaks one language   _____

(4 marks)

2.9 Which of the following long-standing British traditions are now considered to be torture by the European Court of Human Rights?

(a) Morris dancing ☐

(b) Party political broadcasts ☐

(c) World Cup qualification ☐

(d) *The Archers* omnibus edition ☐

(2 marks)

*2.10 In a recent German newspaper poll which of
the following was voted the country's favourite
international goal of all time?*

(a) Maradona, Hand of God
(Argentina v. England 1986) ☐

(b) Maradona, mazy dribble
(Argentina v. England 1986) ☐

(2 marks)

TOTAL MARKS AVAILABLE FOR SECTION II: 24

THE CANDIDATE'S SCORE:

3.1 *Candidates are asked to match the following two short stories with two of Britain's most internationally admired character traits, namely:*

(a) Parsimony ☐   (b) Compassion ☐

(i) A man was delivered to a Blackpool mortuary wearing an expensive, expertly tailored black suit. Bill, the mortician, asked the deceased's wife how she would like the body dressed. He pointed out that the man did look very good in his black suit. The widow, however, said that she always thought her husband looked his best in dark blue. She gave Bill a blank cheque and said, 'I don't care what it costs, but please have my husband in a dark blue suit for the viewing.'

The woman returned the next day. To her delight, she found her husband dressed in a perfect dark-blue suit with a subtle chalk stripe, and the suit fit him perfectly. She said to Bill, 'Whatever the cost, I'm happy. You did an excellent job and I'm very grateful. How much did you spend?'

To her astonishment, Bill returned the blank cheque. 'No charge,' he said.

'No, really, I must pay you for the cost of the suit!' she said.

'Honestly,' Bill said, 'it didn't cost anything. You see, a dead gentleman of about your husband's size was brought in shortly after you left yesterday and he was wearing an attractive dark-blue suit. I asked his wife if she minded him going to his grave wearing a black suit instead and she said it made no difference as long as he looked nice. So I just switched their heads.'

(ii)   An elderly Cardiff man lay seriously ill in his bed. While suffering in agony, he suddenly smelled the aroma of his favourite scones wafting up the stairs.

He gathered all his remaining strength and gingerly lifted himself from the bed. Leaning against the wall, he slowly made his way out of the bedroom. And then, with an even greater effort, he gripped the banister with both hands and made his way one step at a time downstairs.

With laboured breath, he propped himself against the door frame and gazed into the familiar family kitchen. Were it not for the agonising pain he would have thought himself already in heaven, for spread out on the kitchen table were dozens and dozens of his favourite scones.

Was this actually heaven? Or was it one final act of affection from his devoted wife of some fifty years, lovingly seeing to it that he left this cruel world a happy man?

Mustering one final effort, he threw himself towards the scones but only landed on his knees, just short of the groaning table. As his aged and trembling hand rose slowly towards the elusive scones, his wife suddenly appeared from nowhere and rapped his knuckles with her wooden spoon.

'Paws off,' she barked. 'They're for the funeral.'

(4 marks)

3.2 *Hugo lives in Alderley Edgeshire in Manchester and Bingo lives in the nearby but less salubrious neighbourhood, Hulme Side. From the information provided below, which is Hugo's paper round?*

(a) Paper Round A ☐   (b) Paper Round B ☐

Newspaper	Copies	Newspaper	Copies
Daily Telegraph	23	*Daily Star*	50
The Times	10		
The Spectator	8		
Financial Times	6		

(2 marks)

Street Talk: The Credit Crunch's Impact on British Society

3.3 *Which of the following two Street Talks could apply to many of Britain's most senior bankers or ex-bankers?*

(a) 'Despite losing billions of pounds, not one banker has been charged with an offence.'   ☐
    Y. Knott, Perth

(b) 'To conceal their ill-gotten gains, I suspect that many of our disgraced bankers will have set up their offshore bank accounts.'   ☐
    Isla Man, Douglas

(4 marks)

3.4 *Drawing on your knowledge of the British Isles, please fill the gaps in the statements below with the appropriate nationality: Welshmen, Scotsmen, Irishmen and Englishmen:*

Stranded on a desert island:

The two _____ set up a male voice choir.

The two _____ established a government-owned bank.

The two _____ founded three political parties.

The two _____ did nothing until they were formally introduced.

(2 marks)

3.5 *From the economically challenged mining villages of the worked-out Welsh coalfield to the gritty fishing towns of England's east coast, blue-collar Britain has developed an irrepressible affection for country and western songs. Which of the following such songs topped Britain's country music charts in 1990:*

(a) How Can I Miss You When You Won't Go Away?   ☐

(b) I Keep Forgettin' That I Forgot About You   ☐

(c) I'm So Miserable Without You It's Like Having You Here ☐

(4 marks)

3.6 *An evening spent with friends in the pub is an age-old British tradition. In this story, how many suspects did the policeman successfully breathalyse outside the St Albans pub?*

(a) 1 ☐   (b) 0 ☐

An unmarked police car was parked outside a popular St Albans pub. At about 11 p.m., one of the officers noticed Sam, a well-known local with a fondness for his ale, leaving the bar so intoxicated that he could barely walk. As Sam stumbled around the car park for a few minutes, the officers quietly watched his every move while waiting to pounce.

After what seemed like an eternity and trying his keys on five other vehicles, Sam finally found his car, unlocked the door and collapsed behind the wheel. He took several minutes to compose himself. Meanwhile, a number of the pub's other patrons left the bar, said their cheery goodbyes and drove off.

Finally Sam started his car, but he also inadvertently switched on the windscreen wipers and sounded the horn several times. In his confused state he also forgot to switch on the car's headlights.

He then drove the car forward for a few yards then pulled over for several minutes to allow more cars to leave the pub's emptying car park. Finally Sam left the car park, turned left and started to drive gingerly down the main road.

The police officers, having patiently waited all this time for their unsuspecting prey, gave chase complete with their blue flashing lights and signalled Sam to pull over. He was immediately breathalysed but, to the officers' amazement, the result was negative. Turning to Sam, one officer said, 'I'll have to ask you to accompany me to the station, as our equipment must be faulty.'

'I doubt it,' smiled Sam mischievously. 'I'm tonight's designated decoy.'

(2 marks)

3.7 Does Jack have a point?

(a) Yes ☐   (b) No ☐   (c) Only in Bury ☐

A Bury lad and his sweetheart were sitting on a bench holding hands in the local park, contentedly gazing out across the town's colourful flowerbeds. For several minutes they sat silently. Then finally the girl looked at the boy and said, 'A penny for your thoughts, Jack.'

'Well, uh, I was thinking . . . perhaps it's time for a little kiss?'

The girl blushed, then leaned over and pecked him delicately on the cheek. Jack then blushed also and the two turned once again to gaze out across the park. Minutes passed until the girl spoke once more. 'Another penny for your thoughts, Jack.'

'Well, I was thinking that perhaps it's now time for a little cuddle?'

The girl blushed once again, then leaned over and cuddled him for a few seconds. Once more Jack blushed and then the two returned to their awkward silence.

After a while, she said, 'Yet another penny for your thoughts, Jack.'

'Well, uh . . . I was thinking maybe it's time that you let me put a hand on your leg.'

The girl blushed, then took his hand and put it on her knee. In return, Jack blushed. Then the two turned once again to stare across the park until the girl spoke again. 'Another penny for your thoughts, Jack.'

But this time the young man glanced down with a furrowed brow. 'Well,' he said. 'My thoughts are a bit more serious this time.'

'Really?' responded the girl in a whisper laced with anticipation.

'Yes,' said Jack, nodding nervously.

The girl looked away, began to blush, and bit her lip, impatient for Jack's next request.

After what seemed like an age, Jack stammered, 'Do you not think it's about time you paid me the money you owe me?!'

(2 marks)

3.8 Which one of the people photographed below earns over £250,000 per week and yet as often as not still seems unhappy with their lot in life?

(a) ☐

(b) ☐

(c) ☐

(d) ☐

© iStockphoto

© Shutterstock

© Getty

© Getty

(2 marks)

3.9 *From the exchange presented below, who was surprised most of all?*

(a) Charlie ☐

(b) The policeman ☐

(c) Charlie's wife ☐

Charlie was walking through Blackburn town centre late at night on his way home when he saw a woman lurking in the shadows.

'Twenty quid,' she whispered to Charlie.

Charlie had never been with a lady of the evening before but decided that he would try anything once. Besides, it was only twenty pounds and so they adjourned to the bushes in a nearby park.

The action was only just beginning when all of a sudden a light flashed on them. They had been discovered by the police!

'What's going on here?' asked the officer.

'I'm making love to my wife,' Charlie answered, quick as a flash and sounding mildly irritated at the interruption.

'Oh, I am sorry,' replied the policeman. 'I didn't realise.'

'Well, neither did I,' replied Charlie, 'till you shone that torch in her face!'

(2 marks)

TOTAL MARKS AVAILABLE FOR SECTION III: 24

THE CANDIDATE'S SCORE:

4.1 *A humorous contradiction in terms, more properly known as an oxymoron, is one of the many delights of the British language. Which of the following such expressions won the coveted 'Harsh But Fair' award at the recent Camelot University conference on the subject?*

(a) Understanding judge ☐   (d) Greenwich University ☐

(b) Karaoke singer ☐   (e) Religious tolerance ☐

(c) Solvent bank ☐   (f) Communist Party ☐

(2 marks)

4.2 *Many observers believe that malapropisms[1] appear to have been invented specifically for some of the country's more confused politicians. Which of the following statements are largely thought to be genuine as opposed to playful urban myths?*

(a) 'Certain allegations have been made against me and when I catch these alligators . . .' ☐

(b) 'After my poor election showing, it may not be much of a constipation, but at least I didn't lose my deposit.' ☐

(c) 'UKIP's popularity is beyond my apprehension.' ☐

[1] Malapropism: creating a ridiculous effect by mistakenly using a word in place of a similar-sounding one.

(2 marks)

4.3 *Is there a spelling mistake in the illustration below?*

(a) Yes ☐   (b) No ☐   (c) Yes and no ☐

Jock out the Box, July 7ᵗʰ 2013

(2 marks)

4.4 *What is the technically correct term for a small Oxford professor sandwiched between two fighting football fans?*

(a) Short-sighted ☐   (c) Toast ☐

(b) Invisible ☐   (d) An interpreter ☐

(2 marks)

4.5 *The British male has an enviable reputation for engaging the ladies in conversation and for quick-witted banter. Which of the following pub-based quotes represents the British male at his most engaging best?*

(a) 'Are you going to finish that drink?' ☐

(b) 'I want you to have my children – they're in the car outside.' ☐

(2 marks)

4.6 *The English language is always evolving and innovative. Please consider which of the following recent nominations for inclusion in the Oxford English Dictionary you could see yourself using once settled in Britain:*

(a) **Cashtration:** (n) What most Brits feel as the end of the month approaches ☐

(b) **Ignoranus:** (n) A jobsworth who's both stupid and an ass ☐

(c) **Foreploy:** (n) Any male strategy devised solely for the purpose of getting sex ☐

(d) **Coffee:** (n) Home Counties word for the person upon whom one coughs ☐

(e) **Frackas:** (n) A noisy public protest against fracking ☐

(f) **Farage:** (v) To lead a group of swivel-eyed loons ☐

(4 marks)

4.7 *Could Birmingham's solution (see below) help out other UK cities with a thick local accent?*

(a) Yes ☐   (b) No ☐

(2 marks)

4.8 *What is the appropriate term for a beautiful woman with a beer-bellied Geordie?*

(a) Blind   ☐   (c) Mismatched   ☐

(b) Desperate ☐   (d) A hostage   ☐

(2 marks)

4.9 Please match the following four new Andy Murray words and their associated definitions to the illustrations presented below:

(a) **Murrayhome:** To leave work early and rush home to watch Murray on TV ☐

(b) **Andyrexic:** The teenage Murray ☐

(c) **Andycedents:** British tennis players before Murray ☐

(d) **Andymonium:** Wimbledon Centre Court, Sunday, 7 July 2013, 5.20 p.m. ☐

(4 marks)

4.10 Is the British definition of a heatwave:

(a) A Spanish holiday ☐

(b) The menopause ☐

(c) A two-bar electric fire ☐

(2 marks)

TOTAL MARKS AVAILABLE FOR SECTION IV: 24

THE CANDIDATE'S SCORE:

5.1 Does Young Tom make your heart swell with pride?

(a) Absolutely ☐   (b) Absolutely ☐

The only way for the Williamsons to find time for a Sunday afternoon 'quickie' with their son, the ever-inquisitive Young Tom, hanging around was to send him out on the balcony with a Mars Bar and then ask the lad to deliver a running commentary on the goings-on in the street below.

On this particular Sunday, Young Tom, placated with a Mars bar as usual, soon began his commentary and his parents put their plan into action.

'The Andersons have visitors.'

'David is out riding his bike again.'

'Andy's on his skateboard.'

'Sam and his brother are playing football.'

'Mary's taking her dog for a walk.'

'The Coopers are shagging!'

Startled, both parents shot up in bed and the flustered dad asked, 'Tom, how do you know what they're doing?'

'Because Jimmy Cooper's out on his balcony eating a Mars Bar!'

(2 marks)

5.2 *Which of the following names were not considered as suitable for the new royal prince?*

(a) Cletus ☐   (d) Jedward ☐

(b) Rex ☐   (e) Del Boy ☐

(c) Gangnam ☐   (f) Bismark ☐

(4 marks)

5.3 *The often reproduced photograph below is of:*

(a) Prince Harry ☐   (c) Julian Clary ☐

(b) Mel Gibson ☐   (d) Alex Salmond ☐

(4 marks)

© Superstock

5.4 *On 4 June 1977 (see photograph below) London was invaded by:*

(a) Romans ☐

(b) Vikings ☐

(c) Goths ☐

(d) Glaswegians ☐

(4 marks)

© PA

5.5 *Based on the illustration below, are Britain's doctors correct to conclude that the country's obesity problem will eventually sort itself out?*

(a) Yes ☐   (b) No ☐

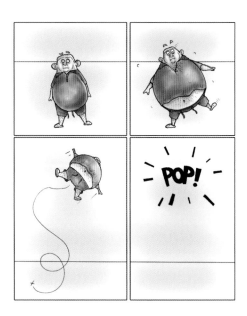

(4 marks)

5.6 *Britain recently developed a new missile system. Sadly the weapon rarely worked and could not be fired. From the options listed below, please select what you think was the missile's codename:*

(a) Civil Service ☐   (b) House of Lords ☐

(2 marks)

5.7 *In the Royal Family's dictionary, 'estimate' means:*

(a) The Queen's horse that won the 2013 Ascot Gold Cup ☐

(b) The figure Prince Charles puts on the Duchy of Cornwall's tax return ☐

(2 marks)

TOTAL MARKS AVAILABLE FOR SECTION V: 22

THE CANDIDATE'S SCORE:

GEOGRAPHY

6.1 *Candidates are asked to decide why the Cornish encounter described below is fictional. Is it because:*

(a) Mermaids don't exist ☐

(b) Mermaids can't talk ☐

An Englishman, a Scotsman and an Irishman were walking along a remote beach in Cornwall when suddenly they came across a mermaid. They immediately struck up a playful conversation.

The Scotsman asked whether the mermaid had ever been kissed. She blushed and said no, so the Scotsman kissed her and she giggled.

Taking up the challenge, the Englishman then asked her if she'd ever been fondled. The mermaid blushed and said no, so the Englishman duly obliged and she giggled.

The brave Irishman then asked if she'd ever been shafted. The mermaid blushed and said no. The Irishman said, 'Well, you have now, the tide's gone out.'

(2 marks)

Street Talk: Global Warming

6.2 *Which of the following comments about the impact of global warming on Britain do you agree with?*

(a) 'Climatic changes are unpredictable.' ☐
Elle Nino, Preston

(b) 'Are you sure that we will not miss the wet weather?' ☐
Wayne E. Days, Blackpool

(2 marks)

6.3 *Having read the passage below, should shark fishing be legal in Britain?*

(a) Yes ☐   (b) No ☐

On a rare visit to Liverpool, the Queen took some time off to visit Antony Gormley's famous 'Another Place' sculptures stretched out along nearby Crosby beach. Her Majesty's Range Rover was driving along the golden sands when she heard a commotion. The Queen and her entourage rushed to see what was happening, and on approaching the scene she noticed that just beyond the surf there was a hapless man wearing nothing but a Manchester United football top and frantically struggling to free himself from the jaws of a twenty-foot-long shark!

Suddenly a speedboat with three men wearing Liverpool tops sped into view. One of the men took aim at the shark and fired a harpoon into its ribs, immobilising the predator instantly. The other two reached out and pulled the Manchester United fan from the water, and then, using nothing more than their bare hands, they beat the shark to death.

Having bundled the semi-conscious man and the dead shark into the speedboat, they were preparing to speed off when they saw the Queen beckoning to them from the shore. Not wishing to appear rude, the lads beached their boat and went to see the monarch. The Queen went into raptures about the rescue and said, 'I heard that some football fans in this area were sworn enemies, but I've just witnessed a truly enlightened example of bipartisan harmony that should serve as a model for other British teams.'

Overwhelmed by what she had just seen, the Queen knighted them all on the spot and then drove off feeling uplifted by the selfless example shown by her ever-loyal subjects. As she departed, the bemused harpoonist asked the others, 'What was that all about?!'

'That,' one answered, 'was our long-serving Queen and remarkably she knows everything about Britain.'

'Well,' the harpoonist replied, 'she knows nothing about shark fishing. How's our bait holding up? Or should we get a fresh one?'

(2 marks)

6.4 Which of the following are the actual names of towns in England?

(a) Friars Entry ☐   (d) Nether Regions ☐

(b) Lower Swell ☐   (e) Little Cockup ☐

(c) Blind Fiddler ☐   (f) Great Cockup ☐

(4 marks)

6.5 What is happening in the picture below?

(a) Digital fleecing ☐   (b) Roaming in the gloaming ☐

Breaking news....... Tourist visiting London faces bankruptcy over his roaming charges

(2 marks)

6.6 Which, if any, was a former British colony?

(a) Bora Bora ☐   (b) Bunga Bunga ☐

(c) Bongo Bongo ☐

(4 marks)

6.7 *Global warming is expected to have a profound influence on wildlife throughout Britain. From the two sets of photographs presented below, is the left-hand set of images:*

(a) Pre global warming ☐   (b) Post global warming ☐

Puffins, Anglesey

The Animal Shelter, Doncaster

Birds of prey, Snowdonia

Shetland ponies, Brecon Beacons

(4 marks)

6.8 *What is conceptually wrong with the illustration below?*

Cows Week, Isle of Wight

ANSWER:

(2 marks)

*6.9   In Fermanagh, Northern Ireland, distance is always
       measured in minutes, so what is time measured in?*

ANSWER:

(4 marks)

TOTAL MARKS AVAILABLE FOR SECTION VI: 26

THE CANDIDATE'S SCORE:

Examiner's Note: *To appease the ever-restless Scots, the Examination Board has decided that this great (if at times slightly ungrateful) ethnic minority should have its own 'devolved' section. Candidates not interested in emigrating to Scotland may skip this part of the paper and award themselves 18 marks, a score of 75%.*

7.1 *As candidates are no doubt aware, Scotland's lacklustre footballing performance over the last twenty years has left many Scottish males profoundly depressed. Thankfully, the sport of Saxonfreude[1] was developed by psychologists at Invernecky University and the game of Saxon baiting has boosted Scottish self-esteem ever since. Which of the following images can be found in Edinburgh's new National Gallery of Saxonfreude?*

[1] *Saxonfreude is an old Gaelic word for taking pleasure in the misfortunes of Saxons, aka the English. It is thought that the word is in turn derived from the similar-sounding German word Schadenfreude.*

(a) ☐

(b) ☐

(c) ☐

(d) ☐

(2 marks)

7.2 Male life expectancy in Calton in the East End of Glasgow is only fifty-four, whereas in Chelsea and Kensington it is eighty-four. The thirty-year difference is largely explained by which of the following environmental factors?

(a) Ambushes ☐

(b) A bad pint ☐

(c) The Gulf Stream ☐

(4 marks)

7.3 For most Scots, Edinburgh is most aptly described as:

(a) Approximately forty-two miles east of Glasgow ☐

(b) Fine, once they finish building the other side of Princes Street ☐

(2 marks)

Street Talk: Economic Downturn in Scotland

7.4 Which of the following comments do you believe ring true?

(a) 'There's nothing a small country like Scotland can do about the recession.' ☐
Kaye Serasera, Helensburgh

(b) 'To kick-start the economy, Scotland must export more.' ☐
Sally Forth, Falkirk

(2 marks)

7.5 *Over the last twenty years, what has been Scotland's most successful export?*

(a) Whisky ☐   (c) Andy Murray ☐

(b) Irn Bru ☐   (d) Oil ☐

(2 marks)

7.6 *Which one of the photographs below is a magnified image of the infamous Scottish midge?*

(a) ☐

(b) ☐

(c) ☐

(d) ☐

(2 marks)

Bonus Opporchancity

7.7 *When talking about a Glaswegian what is the anthropological significance of the subtle difference in the spelling of the words 'Weegi' and 'Weegie'?*

(2 marks)

7.8 *From the conversation below, please decide whether Jake's future wife has been sexually active for some time:*

(a) Yes ☐   (b) No ☐

Archie and Jake were sitting in the pub discussing Jake's forthcoming wedding.

'Ach, it's all going magic,' said Jake. 'I've got everything organised already: the flooers, the church, the motors, the reception, the rings, the minister, even ma stag night.'

Archie nodded approvingly.

'I've even bought a kilt to be married in!' continued Jake.

'A kilt!' exclaimed Archie. 'That's a great idea, you'll look really smart in that! And what's the tartan?'

'Och,' said Jake, 'I'd imagine she'll be in white.'

(2 marks)

Bonus Opporchancity

7.9 *Scotland is a patchwork of colourful and evocative dialects. With this in mind, the following tale should be read out loud in Doric, the dialect of north-eastern Scotland. Once candidates have reflected on the passage, they should then decide whether they sympathise with the girl's confusion:*

(a) Yes ☐   (b) No ☐

Two rural Aberdeenshire girls went into Aberdeen to get their passport photos taken. When the very old-fashioned photographer went behind his antique camera and pulled the black cloth hood over his head, the following conversation ensued between the two girls:

'Whit's he daein'?'

'He's jist gonna focus.'

'Whit, baith at the same time?'

(2 marks)

7.10 *Do you believe that the grainy black-and-white photograph reproduced below provides indisputable evidence that the Loch Ness Monster exists?*

(a) Absolutely, never any doubt.   ☐

(b) It's still very difficult to say. It could be a trick of the light, or even just a big branch floating on the loch.   ☐

(2 marks)

7.11 In the SNP's new map of Britain (see below) which place name is misspelled?

No.	Place Name	
1	Auchtermuchtie	☐
2	Auchenshoogle	☐
3	Auchterarder	☐
4	Auchenshuggle	☐
5	Aufurfuksake	☐

(2 marks)

1-4

5

TOTAL MARKS AVAILABLE FOR SECTION VII: 24

THE CANDIDATE'S SCORE:

8.1 Do you believe that the encounter reported below is a true story?

(a) Yes, it happens all the time ☐

(b) No, they've all seen the light ☐

On an infamous banker's return to London in 2012 after a period of self-imposed exile, he was going home in his chauffeur-driven limousine when he saw two men on the roadside verge eating grass. Disturbed, he ordered his driver to stop and he got out to investigate.

He asked one man, 'Why are you eating grass?'

'After the credit crunch and the collapse of the banks we don't have any money for food,' the poor man replied. 'So we have to eat grass.'

'Well, then, you can come with me to my house and I'll feed you,' the banker said.

'But sir, I have a wife and two children with me. They are over there, under that tree.'

'Bring them along as well,' the banker replied. Turning to the other poor man, he stated, 'You can come along with us as well.'

The second man, in a cowed voice, said, 'But sir, I also have a wife and six children with me!'

'Bring them all as well,' the banker answered sympathetically.

They all bundled into the car. Once underway, one of the poor fellows turned to the banker and said, 'Sir, you are too kind. Thank you for taking all of us with you. Now our families will not go hungry.'

The banker smiled thinly and then replied, 'Glad to do the favour. You'll really love my place. I've not been home for a while and the grass is nearly a foot high.'

(4 marks)

8.2 *Since 2008, Britain has suffered a major economic crisis. According to the Guardian newspaper, what was the cause of the recession?*

(a) Margaret Thatcher ☐   (d) Carol Thatcher ☐

(b) Dennis Thatcher ☐   (e) Meryl Streep ☐

(c) Mark Thatcher ☐

(4 marks)

Street Talk: The Recession

8.3 *Which of the following comments do you believe ring true?*

(a) 'If it is to recover, the British economy should focus more on research and development.' ☐
Pat Pending, Bath

(b) 'With the economy still in the doldrums, it's the women who are keeping a stiff upper lip.' ☐
Bo Tox, Cheltenham

(4 marks)

8.4 *Given the illustration below, is it now just too difficult to open a new bank account in Britain?*

(a) Yes ☐   (b) No ☐

The Bank's Account Opening Team grills the toothfairy about her source of funds.

(4 marks)

8.5 *Subject to planning permission, which of the organisations below are thought to be in the running to lease London's iconic Shard building?*

(a) Transport for London ☐

(b) BAE Systems ☐

(c) The Ku Klux Klan (UK) Ltd ☐

(d) Faber-Castell ☐

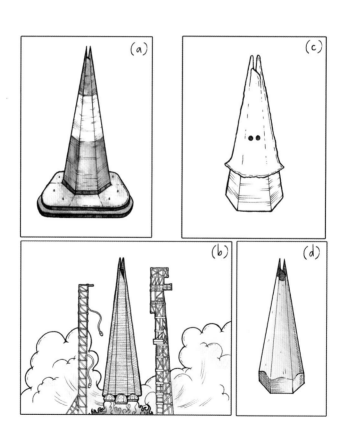

(2 marks)

Street Talk: Bankers

8.6 White of the following Street Talk comments about City bankers do you agree with?

(a) 'Let's hope all the guilty bankers leave soon.'
Oscar Foxtrot, York ☐

(b) 'The media should continue to hound Bob Diamond, Barclays ex-Chief Executive.'
Tilly Emigrates, Hampshire ☐

(c) 'Clearly the regulators were asleep at the wheel as Britain's banking system crashed.'
Toulouse Le Plot, Torquay ☐

(d) 'Bankers are always more concerned about numbers than people.'
Sue Duko, Bishop's Stortford ☐

(2 marks)

TOTAL MARKS AVAILABLE FOR SECTION VIII: 20

THE CANDIDATE'S SCORE:

Warning: this section contains some clichéd and insensitive stereotyping of the Burberry-collared element of British Society.

9.1   In a previous exam, which famous British genius gave the answer for 'find x' shown below?

(a) Prof. Stephen Hawking ☐   (c) Prof. Brian Cox ☐

(b) Stephen Fry ☐   (d) Wayne Rooney ☐

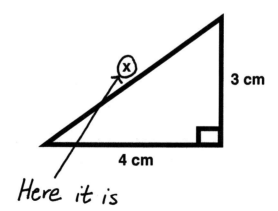

3 cm

4 cm

Here it is

(2 marks)

9.2 *Muzza and Jaffa stole a 2007 green Toyota 1600GL with a mileage of 35,000, and Banjo paid them £1,000 cash in hand for the car. How much more would they have received from Banjo if the car had been a 2008 registration in metallic silver, had only done 19,000 miles and had four new low-profile tyres?*

ANSWER:

(2 marks)

9.3 *Chardonnay's personal trainer only charges £50 a week, but he can have sex with her whenever he wants. Bianca's trainer charges £250 a week and has refused to consider sexual favours as a payment in kind. Which one of the two women weighs nineteen stone and showers infrequently?*

(a) Chardonnay ☐   (b) Bianca ☐

(2 marks)

Bonus Opporchancity

9.4 Barney Baillie bought half a kilo of cocaine for £20,000. By
selling the drugs on his local street corners he hopes to make
100% profit margin on the transaction.

Assuming that Barney and his two associates, Muzza and Jaffa,
consume 10% of the cocaine themselves and that Mad Malky
only takes his standard 10% cut in protection money, how
much must Barney charge per gram to meet his return-on-
investment target?

Candidates may assume cocaine does not attract VAT and, to
avoid any adverse consumer reaction, Barney does not cut his
supply with talcum powder.

(All workings should be clearly shown.)

(2 marks)

9.5 *London's Oxford Street is approximately 2,650 yards
long. If the economically feasible distance between
panhandlers is 100 yards, how many former bankers
can make a living on the street? Candidates may
assume that they all work on the northern side of the
street between the hours of 10 a.m. and 4 p.m., with
two hours off for lunch.*

ANSWER:

(2 marks)

9.6   *Barry faces a dilemma. He believes that he'll get £13.50 in Married Couple's Allowance a week if he finally ties the knot with Chantelle. However, he calculates that even if he managed to borrow the ring and gets the cocaine at a discount from Barney, the wedding will still cost him £250. Worryingly, he'll also have to start buying two curries at £3.50 each every night instead of the one he lives on currently. From a financial perspective, how long will it be before Barry wishes he'd stayed single?*

(a) Immediately ☐   (b) As soon as he sobers up ☐

(4 marks)

9.7   *If in 2012 seven out of every four Yorkshire adults claimed the government's Bereavement Allowance, how many people live in the county?*

(a) 5.3m   ☐   (b) 0   ☐

(c) Minus 5.3m ☐   (d) Other ☐

(2 marks)

Bonus Opporchancity

9.8   When an Englishman moves to France, why does the average IQ of both countries increase? Answer in the space provided and please show your workings.

(4 marks)

9.9 *Magnus from Edinburgh's affluent Morningside area has discovered that 50% of his friends went to school with Ewan McGregor. Another 33% say that their uncle went to Edinburgh University with Gordon Brown. Some 25% say that their dad played against Tony Blair at rugby when he was at Edinburgh's Fettes College, and 20% insist that Sean Connery was the family's milkman.*

Based on this information, what percentage of Magnus's friends claim to know Susan Boyle, the chanteuse from nearby West Lothian?

(a) 0% ☐   (b) 100% ☐

(2 marks)

9.10 *If Jones the farmer laid every sheep in Wales end to end, would he be arrested?*

(a) Absolutely ☐   (b) Whatever for? ☐

(2 marks)

TOTAL MARKS AVAILABLE FOR SECTION IX: 24

THE CANDIDATE'S SCORE:

APPENDIX 1.

THE TEST ANSWERS

I

GENDER STUDIES

1.1 (d) The average British male could never be associated with milk.

1.2 (b) An old soldier would not be drinking a cappuccino, unless perhaps he thought Cappuccino was that big battle he fought in Italy during the spring of 1944. Of course, the old soldier would also have noticed that the abstract Union Flag on page iii looked suspiciously like a reclining nude (see also page 59).

1.3 (c) As there are no rocket scientists or brain surgeons in Penrith.

1.4 (c) Belfast men do cry when ironing but only when also asked to take the rubbish out.

1.5 (b) No! Any Brit called Big Jack would never be scared of his bird.

1.6 Both are incorrect. Relate is a brand of condoms.

1.7 (a) And intriguingly the idea is not under copyright.

1.8 (a) And the same is true for Wormwood Scrubs and Eton.

1.9 All four are correct and award yourself two extra marks if you added:

Essex intellectual seeks kindred spirit to complete the Daily Star crossword.

Note that the Leicester-based Saxon [option (d)] would also require certified accounts for the last three financial years from any candidate hoping to fill his vacancy.

1.10 (a) Yes, except if you have a double-barrelled name.

1.11   (c) And two bonus marks if you agree that Jeremy Clarkson's best-ever quote was 'Speed has never killed anyone. Suddenly becoming stationary, that's what gets you'?

1.12   Again, all are incorrect. The correct answer is 'through the heart', except for bankers, lawyers and VAT inspectors, who don't have said organ.

II

EUROPEAN RELATIONS

2.1 (a) And please see how the Met prepared for the next visit of the Brussels bureaucrat:

© iStockphoto

2.2 (a) However, candidates should bear in mind that, under pending legislation, Brits and the French could never really be 'related' as the story implies.

2.3 (a) And if you answered (b) then Britain is probably not for you.

2.4 (a) But the sailor could have been anyone continental or Mediterranean in appearance.

2.5 (b) But please do not attempt this trick if the lights stay on if your train ever enters a tunnel.

2.6 Neither: the correct answer is in Poland.

2.7 After the UK's performance over Syria, the answer is (b). Two bonus marks if you know how to make French toast.

2.8 As in the order presented. Award yourself two bonus marks if you added 'drunk and on holiday' to explain any Brit who can speak more than one language.

2.9　All of the answers are correct and two bonus marks will be awarded to candidates who also suggested Network Rail journeys or travelling on the Northern Line.

2.10　Neither. This accolade was actually won by Frank Lampard: 'Surely it was over the line ref!' (England v. West Germany 2010)

© PA

III

SOCIOLOGY

3.1   The answers are interchangeable and depend on your perspective on life.

3.2   (b) is Bingo's paper round and, despite the socio-economic distress of many of his customers, he makes 50% more in tips than Hugo does in Alderley Edgeshire.

3.3   Both answers are acceptable, and award yourself two bonus marks if you added the following:

'Once again the City's fat cats have only succeeded in taking from the rich and giving to the poor.'
Robin Hoods, Banchory

3.4   As in the order presented in the question. In the past the two Scotsmen may have formed a football team, but those days are now gone.

3.5   All three songs topped the country music charts in 1990, as did 'If I Had Shot You When I Wanted To I'd Be Out By Now'.

3.6   (b) But sadly Sam was sentenced to 150 hours of community service for obstructing the police.

3.7   (a) Add two bonus marks if you knew that Bury Park is actually in Luton.

3.8   (d) Two bonus marks if you agree with the following tabloid headline of a few years ago: 'Rooney tested positive for a performance-enhancing rug'.

3.9   (a) and (b) and (c), plus the security guards watching on the council's CCTV system.

4.1   All answers are correct and a bonus mark if you also thought of 'adult male' or 'amicable divorce'.

4.2   All three are playful urban myths, and two bonus marks if you added the more recent mythical malaproprism, 'Hopefully the coalition might soon fade into Bolivian.'

4.3   (c) And another bonus mark if you knew that this is how Andy Murray hurt his back.

4.4   (a), (c) and (d). Please note that Oxford professors never think of themselves as either small or invisible.

4.5   Neither! The correct answer is of course: 'I may not be the best-looking guy in here but I am the only one talking to you.'

4.6   (a) If you ticked all the boxes, give yourself four marks, and note that in more and more regions of the UK 'cashtration' applies throughout the entire month and not just as the next payday approaches.

4.7   (a) But not in Glasgow, as the local dialect has yet to be translated.

4.8   All bar (b), as beautiful women are never desperate.

4.9   (a) is 1, (b) is 2, (c) is 3, (d) is 4.

Award yourself two bonus marks if you also knew the following Murray-inspired new word:

Hiphipmurray (v)

The way posh people cheer on Murray at Wimbledon

4.10   (c) is correct if consumers could ever afford to switch it on both bars.

5.1   (a) and (b).

5.2   None was considered suitable, but as a nod to history, Bismark
       (f) was shortlisted as a middle name.

5.3   None of the above. It is, in fact, Alex Ferguson.

5.4   (d) Glaswegians led by Alex Ferguson (see also 5.3 above). Two
       bonus marks if you also pointed out that similar sackings of the
       capital occurred in every second year for the previous century
       yet war was never officially declared between the two countries
       involved.

5.5   (a) Yes, although many citizens may explode before take-off. As
       the illustration below explains, doctors are becoming increasingly
       concerned that any trend towards al fresco dining in a warmer
       Britain may not usher in a Mediterranean-style diet.

5.6   (a) and (b) and two bonus marks if you also suggested Prince
       Andrew.

5.7   (a) and (b) are both correct. Re. Charles, please see the records
       of the 15 July 2013 Public Accounts Committee hearing.

6.1 Neither option is correct. The encounter was fictional, but only because Cornish mermaids never blush when exposed to sexual innuendo.

6.2 Given the masochistic nature of the British personality, the answer is (b).

Two extra marks if you added the following contribution to the debate:

Climatic changes are cyclical, so global warming may only bring short-term benefits to Britain.
Elle Nino, Girvan

6.3 (a) The real question, however, is whether the Republican Party's lunatic fringe believes that it should be legal to hunt the Royal Family.

6.4 All are correct. Candidates should note that, contrary to popular opinion, Cods Wallop and Mucking Fuddle are not names of English towns.

6.5 Both 'digital fleecing' and 'roaming in the gloaming' are being illustrated. The high roaming costs are explained by BT having to recoup the cost of its winning bid of £897 million to screen Championship League and Europa Cup football matches from 2015.

6.6 If you are a certain (ex) UKIP MEP, the answer is (c). For the avoidance of doubt, Wonga Wonga refers to MPs' expenses and is not an offshore island owned by Lord Ashcroft.

6.7 Pre global warming the answer should be (a), but have you ever been to Doncaster's Animal Shelter?

6.8 As cows do not have opposable thumbs, they could not grip the yacht's rudder properly.

6.9 One Guinness equals fifteen minutes.

SCOTTISH STUDIES

7.1 All images except (b) and (d). These two pictures are both to be found hanging in the award-winning Glasgow Gallery of Saxonfreude.

7.2 All are incorrect. The answer is Margaret Thatcher.

7.3 Both are correct. However, in the post-2008 world of the credit crunch, candidates could have added either:

The Athens of the North

The Reykjavik of the South

7.4 Both answers ring true, and two bonus marks if candidates also wrote:

'When times are tough the government should do more to protect Scotland's valuable fishing grounds.'
Fraser Burgh, Fraserborough

7.5 (b) Irn Bru, but up until 2008, the infamous Year of the Shred, the answer would have been banking.

7.6 All options except (b). This is obviously a Dalek, which looks nothing like a midge and could not even hover until 1965 (see 'The Chase', *Doctor Who*).

7.7 Weegi is Protestant and Weegie is Catholic, except in mixed marriages, where the couple would be known as Squeegees.

7.8 (b) No, as the wee rascal Archie knows only too well!

7.9 (a) Candidates, as well as the two girls, should also be confused, as curiously Aberdeen is not, in fact, part of Aberdeenshire.

7.10 (a) Absolutely, never any doubt. What further proof would any reasonable person need?

7.11 (1) 'Auchtermuchtie' should be spelled with a 'y' and not 'ie'.

8.1   (b) Absolutely not, it is merely a cheap joke at the expenses of Britain's beleaguered financial services industry and any similarity with persons either alive or shredded is merely coincidental.

8.2   All five answers are correct – along with the Baroness Thatcher's father Alfred, mother Beatrice, sister Muriel and her two grandchildren, Michael and Amanda.

8.3   Both answers are correct. Two bonus marks if you also thought of:

'Cutting welfare benefits is mean-spirited and will have little or no impact on the UK's budget deficit.'
Penny Pincher

8.4   (a) But try the Isle of Man Bank. Note that the Tooth Fairy remains a central plank of the government's quantitative-easing programme

8.5   All, and two bonus marks if you believe that the Shard would make a good home for both the Department of Education and Random House, a leading publisher of romantic fiction (see below).

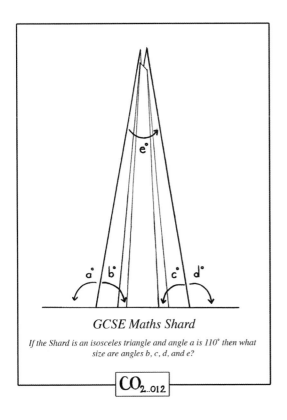

GCSE Maths Shard

If the Shard is an isosceles triangle and angle a is 110° then what size are angles b, c, d, and e?

$CO_{2..012}$

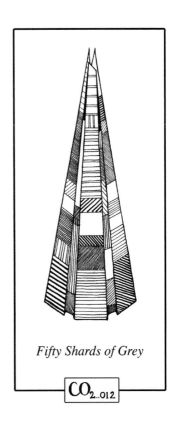

Fifty Shards of Grey

$CO_{2..012}$

8.6   Candidates should agree with all comments and avail themselves of two bonus marks if they also wrote:

'Most people were delighted when Fred Goodwin left the Royal Bank.'
Gladys Allover, Watford

9.1 None of the above. Unfortunately the question should have read:

'Which author wrote "x marks the spot"?' and the answer would have been Robert Louis Stevenson.

9.2 £320, or £450 if a getaway driver is included.

9.3 (b) Logic suggests Bianca, but the question remains: would anyone pay a personal trainer £250 a week and yet still weigh 19 stone?*

* 266 lb if you are American and 120 kg if you are a possible EU appeaser.

9.4 £97.78 per gram, call it £100 to cover 'shrinkage', known on the street as 'the angels' share'.

However, as Barney and his mates are more likely to consume 70% of the cocaine and Mad Malky's cut is more likely to be 20%, the likely cost per gram is £320.

9.5 Given the fees at public schools in England, no more than one.

9.6 Neither. Barry decided it was best never to sober up.

9.7 (d) Where (d) is definitely minus something or other.

9.8 Up until now no social scientist has adequately explained this phenomenon. Curiously, the same result has also been observed when an Englishman moves to Wales. However, when the English move to Scotland the opposite happens.

9.9 (a) 0% up until they saw Susan's bank balance and then it immediately changed to (b), 100%.

9.10 (b) Which, incidentally, is in line with the law throughout the British Isles.

THE BRITISH NATIONALITY TEST

FINAL SCORES[1]

Section		Marks Available	Candidate's Score	Per cent Scored
I	Gender Studies[2]	24		
II	European Relations	24		
III	Sociology	24		
IV	English Language	24		
V	Modern Studies[2]	22		
VI	Geography	26		
VII	Scottish Studies[3]	24		
VIII	Business and Banking	20		
IX	Applied Mathematics	24		
	Bonus Marks Available in the Answers	38		
	TOTAL[4,5]	250		

Notes:

1. As explained in the test's instructions, please adjust your score for either EU sympathies (minus ten) and/or EU culinary leanings (minus fifteen). You may also add other bonus marks as appropriate

2. A minimum of 80% is required in these two sections.

3. If you decided to skip the Scottish section you may award yourself 18 marks (a 75% score).

4. You may also add any bonus marks you picked up in the answers section.

5. Ten bonus marks for spotting the reclining nude on pages iii and 59.

Signed by Candidate:	
Signed by Examiner:	
Witness:	
Date:	

APPENDIX 2.

FREQUENTLY
ASKED QUESTIONS

Q   Do we really have to answer all the questions?

A   No, this is a spoof exam compiled for one of Britain's increasingly rare rainy days.

Q   Will Euro baiting still be legal?

A   Yes, and several of Britain's major universities will offer both undergraduate and postgraduate degrees in the subject. Two prestigious Farage Scholarships will be available for the more gifted students who wish to progress to PhD level in the subject.

Q   If you had left Britain but now wished to return, would that be permitted?

A   Only under special circumstances. However, all such 'previous Brits' will be required to pay higher taxes and must make their home in one of Britain's spartan 'adjustment centres', such as Barnsley or Hull.

Q   Will Geordies lose their distinctive accent?

A   Our experts say that over time the Geordie accent is expected to become more Mediterranean in its delivery. Curiously, Scousers are expected to retain their distinctive accent, especially when overexcited.

Q   As the weather warms, could Britain's flame-haired citizens of Celtic ancestry be threatened with extinction?

A   Not necessarily, as it will be the government's intention to keep citizens with fair complexions and ginger hair indoors during the nine months of summer.

Q   Will greenfly still threaten Britain's roses?

A   No, thankfully greenfly will be a thing of the past, as indeed will roses.

PRAISE FOR THE BRITISH IMMIGRATION INITIATIVE

'They better arrive soon before everyone else has left.'
Di Aspora, *Watford*

'Immigrants have always been welcome in England.'
P.N. Occhio, *Bolton*

'The government should have invited in many more high-calibre immigrants years ago.'
Miss D. Boat and Miss D. Opportunity, *Maidstone*

'We need more immigrants as soon as possible.'
Kitty Exhausted and Owen Billions, *Westminster*